Draw Near with Faith
The Service of Holy Communion
for new Communicants

Draw Near with Faith

*The Service of Holy Communion
for new Communicants*

Raymond Chapman

The Lutterworth Press

Cambridge

The Lutterworth Press
PO Box 60
Cambridge
CB1 2NT

British Library Cataloguing in Publication Data:
A catalogue record for this book is available from the British Library

ISBN 0 7188 2923 9

Copyright © Raymond Chapman 1995

First published by The Lutterworth Press 1995

Printed in Great Britain by
St Edmundsbury Press

Contents

Acknowledgements

Extracts from The Book of Common Prayer, the rights in which are vested in the Crown, are reproduced by permission of the Crown's Patentee, Cambridge University Press. The service follows the order of the Book of Common Prayer as authorised in 1662. There had been previous versions, in 1549 and 1552, and minor amendments at other times. A proposed revision in 1928 was not officially authorised but has been extensively used. Some of its material was used in the Series 1 order for Holy Communion. In most churches there are variations and omissions in the printed order, some of which are noted in this commentary.

The book is illustrated throughout by the work of Nicola Spoor. The cover photograph of the Communion Service at Southwark Cathedral is reproduced here with the kind permission of Cephas Photograph Library. Thanks go to the Rev J Sheldon and to the congregation at St Andrews Chesterton for their help in providing source material for some of the illustrations.

Introduction

You are coming to the most important and special of all Church services. It may be called Holy Communion, Eucharist, Mass or the Lord's Supper. In this service we are doing what Jesus commanded His followers to do in remembrance of Him. In the Gospels we read about the Last Supper which He had with His disciples on the night before He was crucified. He gave them bread and wine, saying THIS IS MY BODY and THIS IS MY BLOOD.

These are the words which the priest uses at every Holy Communion service. If you have been confirmed, you will join the other worshippers in receiving the bread and wine as Christians all over the world have done ever since the days of the Apostles. If you are not yet confirmed, you will join in the rest of the service and will come forward at the time of communion to receive a blessing.

The service may be in the main part of the church, with hymns and a sermon and perhaps several people assisting the priest. It may be said in a quiet side chapel with not many people present. It is always the same service, in which God's people come to offer their love and obedience. Never worry about knowing exactly what to do in the service. Do as others do and remember that we are coming before our loving God, who asks only that we offer our own love to Him.

Some of the words used in the service may seem difficult at first, but your parish priest will be able to explain them, if you have not already learned about them in Confirmation classes, and they will soon become familiar. Words which may be new to you are explained in a glossary at the end of this

The Last Supper, when Jesus gave His disciples bread and wine, saying THIS IS MY BODY and THIS IS MY BLOOD. We recall this event at every Communion service.

book. We are all used to learning new words for special purposes, as for instance in working with computers. For hundreds of years people have found the words of this service both beautiful and prayerful, and now that you are coming to Holy Communion, it is good to become familiar with them.

The words of the service are most important, but there is meaning also in the things that are used. We need to know their names and become accustomed to seeing them, remembering always that what really matters is our loving obedience in this service to what Jesus commanded.

There must always be a priest to lead the service of Holy Communion. He is called the *celebrant* and we say that as he conducts the service he *celebrates*. He may be assisted by one or more other clergy and perhaps by lay people. The celebrant will may be dressed as in the illustration on the right in a surplice and cassock, or as in the illustrations over the page.

His big outer garment is a *chasuble* and its colour will vary according to the season or special holy days. Underneath this he has a *stole* hanging in front over an *alb* which is fastened with a *girdle*.

Celebrants from different churches may be dressed in different vestments. This priest wears a cassock and surplice. Others are shown overleaf.

The Dalmatic / Tunicle.

If a priest assists him, he will also have an alb and stole, and possibly a different outer garment called a *dalmatic* or a *tunicle*, of the same colour as the chasuble. Lay assistants usually wear albs.

The celebrant may instead wear a *surplice* over a *cassock*, as he does for Mattins and Evensong, with a stole or perhaps a black scarf.

The celebrant takes the service as the leader of all those present. He speaks for them to God, and speaks God's word to them. The people will join aloud in some of the words of the service. Even when only the celebrant is speaking, we are all praying silently with him.

This little book will help you to follow the service and to know when to join in. When you see the word *People* before a part of the service, it is a signal to say the words aloud. These passages are printed in **darker type like this**. When the word *Amen* is in bold capital letters like this, **AMEN**, you should say it aloud. It means that we have followed the prayer that has just been said and are asking God to accept it. The word *Priest* before other words of the service means that the celebrant alone says them.

The Chasuble – the colour of this outer garment varies according to the season or holy day.

Before the service

When you get to your place, kneel down and thank God for letting you be there, and ask Him to help you to make a good communion. Then sit quietly until the celebrant and any other ministers enter. If it is a sung service, there will probably be a hymn as they come in. If you have stood for a hymn, kneel again for the beginning of the service. The celebrant goes to the table on which he will celebrate the Holy Communion. We can call it the altar, or the holy table, or the Lord's table. The name is not important and the one word *altar* will be used in this book. The Priest may stand in front of the altar for a short time and say some words of preparation with the others, or he may go straight into the service. When he is ready, he will stand at the middle of the altar, either facing the people or with his back to them. Then the service itself begins.

Altars vary from church to church.

The Service of Holy Communion

The priest alone says quietly:

Our Father which art in heaven,
Hallowed be thy Name.
Thy kingdom come.
Thy will be done,
in earth as it is in heaven.
Give us this day our daily bread.
And forgive us our trespasses,
As we forgive them that trespass against us.
And lead us not into temptation;
But deliver us from evil.
Amen.

We do not join in, because this is still part of his own preparation for celebrating. Then he says a prayer to prepare all the people; usually he says it alone, though in some churches today the people say it with him:

Almighty God,
unto whom all hearts be open, all desires known,
and from whom no secrets are hid;
Cleanse the thoughts of our hearts
by the inspiration of thy Holy Spirit,
that we may perfectly love thee,
and worthily magnify thy holy Name;
through Christ our Lord.
AMEN

The Priest says the Ten Commandments. After each commandment the People say:
Lord, have mercy upon us, and incline our hearts to keep this law.
but after the last one they say:
Lord, have mercy upon us, and write all these thy laws in our hearts, we beseech thee.

Instead of the Ten Commandments, the Priest may say:
Our Lord Jesus Christ said: Hear O Israel, the Lord our God is one Lord; and thou shalt love the Lord thy God with all thy heart, and with all thy soul, and with all thy mind, and with all thy strength. This is the first commandment. And the second is like, namely this: Thou shalt love thy neighbour as thyself. There is none other commandment greater than these. On these two commandments hang all the Law and the Prophets.

The people say:

Lord, have mercy upon us, and incline our hearts to keep this law.

or we may have:

Priest:	*Lord have mercy*
People:	**Christ have mercy**
Priest:	*Lord have mercy*

Whichever words are used, we are asking God to help us to keep His Law and to live as He wants us to live.

The commandments are often followed by a prayer for the Queen:

Almighty God, whose kingdom is everlasting, and power infinite; Have mercy upon the whole Church; and so rule the heart of thy chosen Servant ELIZABETH, our Queen and Governor, that she (knowing whose minister she is) may above all things seek thy honour and glory: and that we and all her subjects (duly considering whose authority she hath) may faithfully serve, honour, and humbly obey her, in thee and for thee, according to thy blessed Word and ordinance; through Jesus Christ our Lord, who with thee and the Holy Ghost liveth and reigneth, ever one God, world without end. **AMEN**

or

Almighty and everlasting God, we are taught by thy holy Word, that the hearts of Kings are in thy rule and governance, and that thou dost dispose and turn them as it seemeth good to thy godly wisdom: We humbly beseech thee so to dispose and govern the heart of ELIZABETH thy servant, our Queen and Governor, that in all her thoughts, words, and works, she may ever seek thy honour and glory, and study to preserve thy people committed to her charge, in wealth, peace, and godliness, for thy dear Son's sake, Jesus Christ our Lord. **AMEN**

Gospel reading.

Then the Priest says a short prayer. This is called the *Collect* because it collects or draws together some special thoughts for the service. There is a collect for every Sunday in the year, which is used through the following week unless there is a Saint's Day.

We sit while the Priest or perhaps one of the other ministers reads a piece from the Bible. This is the Epistle and is usually taken from a letter written by St Paul or one of the other apostles. The reader begins by saying where the Epistle is to be found in the Bible, and at the end says:

Here endeth the Epistle.

We all stand for the Gospel. Before it is read there may be a Psalm or hymn if the service is being sung. The reader of the Gospel says:

The holy Gospel is written in the . . . Chapter of the Gospel according to St . . . , beginning at the . . . Verse

The People say:

Glory be to thee, O Lord

and at the end they say:

Praise be to thee, O Christ

We remain standing and all together say the words of the Creed to declare our faith:

I believe in one God the Father Almighty, Maker of heaven and earth, And of all things visible and invisible: And in one Lord Jesus Christ, the only-begotten Son of God, Begotten of his Father before all worlds, God of God, Light of Light, Very God of very God, Begotten not made, Being of one substance with the Father, By whom all things were made: Who for us men, and for our salvation came down from heaven, And was incarnate by the Holy Ghost of the Virgin Mary, And was made man, And was crucified also for us under Pontius Pilate. He suffered and was buried, And the third day he rose again according to the Scriptures, And ascended into heaven, And sitteth on the right hand of the Father. And he shall come again with glory to judge both the quick and the dead: Whose kingdom shall have no end. And I believe in the Holy Ghost, The Lord and giver of life, Who proceedeth from the Father and the Son, Who with the Father and Son together is worshipped and glorified, Who spake by the Prophets. And I

believe one Catholick and Apostolick Church. I acknowledge one Baptism for the remission of sins. And I look for the Resurrection of the dead, And the life of the world to come. AMEN

At the end of the Creed the Priest may ask us to sit while he gives out notices and perhaps preaches a sermon. We listen carefully to the sermon, and try to learn something from it to help us in our lives as Christians.

After this, or just after the Creed if there are no notices or sermon, the Priest will read a sentence from the Bible. This will probably be:

Let your light so shine before men, that they may see your good works, and glorify your Father which is in heaven.

While the Priest and those assisting him are preparing for the rest of the service, there will probably be a collection of money for the work of the church. If the service is being sung, there will be a hymn at this point. If there is no hymn we can sit and prepare ourselves for the most important part of the service. We may be able to watch what the Priest is doing and we can pray for him as he prepares.

Already on the altar or on a table at the side there will be the plate and cup for the communion, covered with a cloth called the *veil* on which there is placed the *burse*. The veil and burse, and the cloth in front of the altar, the *frontal*, will be the same colour as the chasuble and stole which the Priest is wearing.

From the burse the Priest takes a small white cloth, the *corporal*, and lays it in the middle of the altar. He sets the burse and veil to one side. Under them are the plate and cup used for the communion; the plate is called the *paten* and the cup is the *chalice*. They are important objects because they

*The Chalice
and the Paten
(the paten rests
on top).*

The Ciborium.

represent the plate and cup which Jesus used at the Last Supper. The priest removes a stiff piece of card, the *pall*, from the paten on which there is already a large wafer for his communion. He adds as many wafers as will be needed for the communion of the People. If there are many communicants he will probably put these wafers into a covered cup called a *ciborium*. In some churches a piece of ordinary bread is used. He then pours enough wine, and a little water, into the chalice and puts the pall on top.

He washes his hands to show that he wants God to make him really clean and pure for the wonderful thing which he is going to do. He stands at the middle of the altar and we all kneel. He may mention particular people and needs for inclusion in our prayers and then he says:

Let us pray for the whole state of Christ's Church militant here in earth.

This is the prayer which draws together all that we want to bring before God. The Church Militant consists of all the Christian people who are now living, and we join our prayers with those who have died and are part of the Church Triumphant in heaven.

Almighty and everliving God, who by thy holy Apostle hast taught us to make prayers, and supplications, and to give thanks, for all men; We humbly beseech thee most mercifully to accept our alms and oblations, and to receive these our prayers, which we offer unto thy Divine Majesty; beseeching thee to inspire continually the universal Church with the spirit of truth, unity, and concord: And grant, that all they that do confess thy holy Name may agree in the truth of thy holy Word, and live in unity, and godly love. We beseech thee also to save and defend all Christian Kings, Princes, and Governors; and specially thy servant ELIZABETH our Queen; that under her we may be godly and quietly governed: And grant unto her whole Council, and to all that are put in authority under her, that they may truly and indifferently minister justice, to the punishment of wickedness and vice, and to the maintenance of thy true religion, and virtue. Give grace, O heavenly Father, to all Bishops and Curates, that they may both by their life and doctrine set forth thy true and lively Word, and rightly and duly administer thy holy Sacraments: And to all thy people give thy heavenly grace; and specially to this congregation here present; that, with meek heart and due reverence, they may hear, and receive thy holy Word; truly serving thee in holiness and righteousness all the days of their life. And we most humbly beseech thee of thy goodness, O Lord, to comfort and succour all them, who in this transitory life are in trouble, sorrow, need, sickness, or any other adversity. And we also bless thy holy Name for all thy servants departed this life in thy faith and fear; beseeching thee to give us grace so to follow their good examples, that with them we may be partakers of thy heavenly kingdom: Grant this, O Father, for Jesus Christ's sake, our only Mediator and Advocate. **AMEN**

Then we remember that we do not always obey God, and before we share the Holy Communion we say we are sorry for our sins.

The priest says:

Ye that do truly and earnestly repent you of your sins, and are in love and charity with your neighbours, and intend to lead a new life, following the commandments of God, and walking from henceforth in his holy ways; Draw near with faith, and take this holy Sacrament to your comfort; and make your humble confession to Almighty God, meekly kneeling upon your knees.

Then, kneeling, we all say together:

Almighty God, Father of our Lord Jesus Christ, Maker of all things, Judge of all men; We acknowledge and bewail our manifold sins and wickedness, Which we from time to time, most grievously have committed, By thought, word, and deed, Against thy Divine Majesty, Provoking most justly thy wrath and indignation against us. We do earnestly repent, And are heartily sorry for these our misdoings; The remembrance of them is grievous unto us; The burden of them is intolerable. Have mercy upon us, Have mercy upon us, most merciful Father; For thy Son our Lord Jesus Christ's sake, Forgive us all that is past; And grant that we may ever hereafter Serve and please thee in newness of life, To the honour and glory of thy Name; Through Jesus Christ our Lord. AMEN

The Priest assures us that God forgives us whenever we turn to Him in love:

Almighty God, our heavenly Father, who of his great mercy hath promised forgiveness of sins to all them that with hearty repentance and true faith turn unto him; Have mercy upon you; pardon and deliver you from all your sins; confirm and strengthen you in all goodness; and bring you to everlasting life; through Jesus Christ our Lord. **AMEN**

He says some words from the New Testament; they are 'comfortable' in making us feel more secure, but the real meaning of 'comfortable' here is that they should strengthen us in our Christian lives:

Hear what comfortable words our Saviour Christ saith unto all that truly turn to him.

Come unto me all that travail and are heavy laden, and I will refresh you.

So God loved the world, that he gave his only-begotten Son, to the end that all who believe in him should not perish, but have everlasting life.

Hear also what Saint Paul saith.

This is a true saying, and worthy of all men to be received, That Christ Jesus came into the world to save sinners.

Come unto me . . .

Hear also what Saint John saith.

If any man sin, we have an Advocate with the Father, Jesus Christ the righteous, and he is the propitiation for our sins.

Now we are ready to come to the greatest part of the service:

Priest: *Lift up your hearts.*

People: **We lift them up unto the Lord.**

Priest: *Let us give thanks unto our Lord God.*

People: **It is meet and right so to do.**

Priest: *It is very meet, right, and our bounden duty, that we should at all times, and in all places, give thanks unto thee, O Lord, Holy Father, Almighty, Everlasting God. Therefore with Angels and Archangels, and with all the company of heaven, we laud and magnify thy glorious Name; evermore praising thee, and saying:*

People: **Holy, holy, holy, Lord God of hosts, heaven and earth are full of thy glory: Glory be to thee, O Lord most High. AMEN**

Lift up your hearts.

At special times of the year like Easter and Christmas there will be some extra words before 'Therefore with angels and archangels . . . '

We pause for a moment to remember again that we can receive the Holy Communion not for anything good in us but only because of God's love, and in obedience to His command.

The Priest kneels and says for all present:

We do not presume to come to come to this thy Table, O merciful Lord, trusting in our own righteousness, but in thy manifold and great mercies. We are not worthy so much as to gather up the crumbs under thy Table. But thou art the same Lord, whose property is always to have mercy: Grant us therefore, gracious Lord, so to eat the flesh of thy dear Son Jesus Christ, and to drink his blood, that our sinful bodies may be made clean by his body, and our souls washed through his most precious blood, and that we may evermore dwell in him, and he in us. AMEN.

(In some churches all the people say this prayer together.)

The Priest at the centre of the altar.

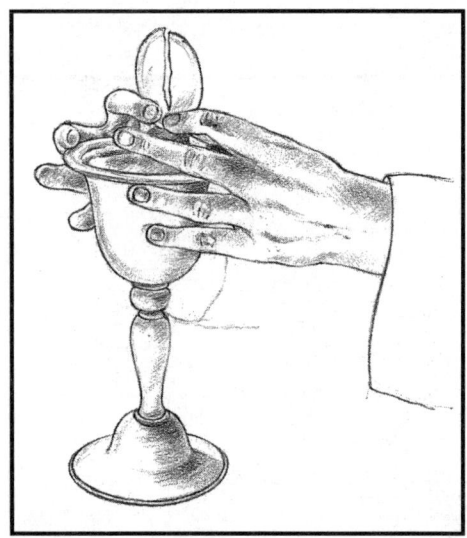

The Breaking of the Bread. The Celebrant may use a wafer, like the one above, or he may break real bread.

Now comes the Prayer of Consecration which includes the words of Jesus at the Last Supper and asks that we may share in the gift of His Body and Blood. The priest stands at the centre of the altar and says:

Almighty God, our heavenly Father, who of thy tender mercy didst give thine only Son Jesus Christ to suffer death upon the cross for our redemption; who made there (by his one oblation of himself once offered) a full, perfect, and sufficient sacrifice, oblation, and satisfaction, for the sins of the whole world; and did institute, and his holy Gospel command us to continue, a perpetual memory of that his precious death, until his coming again; Hear us, O merciful Father, we most humbly beseech thee; and grant that we receiving these thy creatures of bread and wine, according to thy Son our Saviour Jesus Christ's holy institution, in remembrance of his death and passion, may be partakers of his most precious Body and Blood: who, in the same night that he was betrayed, took Bread;

Now the Priest takes up the paten from the altar
and, when he had given thanks, he brake it,
he takes the large wafer and breaks it
and gave it to his disciples, saying, Take, eat, this is my Body which is given for you:
he lays his hand on all the wafers or bread to be given in communion
Do this in remembrance of me. Likewise after supper he took the Cup;
he picks up the chalice
and, when he had given thanks, he gave it to them, saying, Drink ye all of this; for this is my Blood of the New Testament, which is shed for you and for many for the remission of sins:
he lays his hand on the chalice, and on any other chalices which are to be used in communion
Do this, as oft as ye shall drink it, in remembrance of me. AMEN.

When the Priest and any who are assisting him have

Kneeling at the altar rail. Here someone is receiving the Sacrament and someone who has not yet been confirmed is receiving a blessing.

made their communion, the people come forward in turn and kneel at the rail.

As the Priest gives the bread to each communicant, he says some or all of these words:

The Body of our Lord Jesus Christ, which was given for thee, preserve thy body and soul unto everlasting life. Take and eat this in remembrance that Christ died for thee, and feed on him in thy heart by faith with thanksgiving.

When he gives the cup he says some or all of these words:

The Blood of our Lord Jesus Christ, which was shed for thee, preserve thy body and soul unto everlasting life. Drink this in remembrance that Christ's Blood was shed for thee, and be thankful.

If you have been confirmed you will have been told how to receive the bread and wine. If you are not yet confirmed, keep your hands down and bow your head for a blessing. Return to your place, kneel, and thank God for His love and mercy.

When all have communicated, the priest washes the

The washing of the vessels.

sacred vessels and puts them aside; he may do this at the end of the service instead, perhaps during the last hymn if there is one.

We all say together the prayer which Jesus taught us to say:
Our Father, which art in heaven, Hallowed by thy Name. Thy kingdom come. Thy will be done, in earth as it is in heaven. Give us this day our daily bread. And forgive us our trespasses, As we forgive them that trespass against us. And lead us not into temptation; But deliver us from evil: For thine is the kingdom, The power, and the glory, For ever and ever. AMEN.

The Priest says one of the following prayers.
O Lord and heavenly Father, we thy humble servants entirely desire thy fatherly goodness mercifully to accept this our sacrifice of praise and thanksgiving; most humbly beseeching thee to grant, that by the merits and death of thy Son Jesus Christ, and through faith in his blood, we and all thy whole Church may obtain remission of our sins, and all other benefits of his passion. And here we offer and present unto thee, O Lord, ourselves, our souls and bodies, to be a reasonable, holy, and lively sacrifice unto thee; humbly beseeching thee, that all we, who are partakers of this holy Communion, may be fulfilled with thy grace and heavenly benediction. And although we be unworthy, through our manifold sins, to offer unto thee any sacrifice, yet we beseech thee to accept this our bounden duty and service; not weighing our merits, but pardoning our offences, through Jesus Christ our Lord; by whom, and with whom, in the unity of the Holy Ghost, all honour and glory be unto thee, O Father Almighty, world without end. **AMEN**

or

Almighty and everliving God, we most heartily thank thee, for that thou dost vouchsafe to feed us, who have duly received these holy mysteries, with the spiritual food of the most precious Body and Blood of thy Son our Saviour Jesus Christ; and dost assure us thereby of thy favour and goodness towards us; and that we are very members incorporate in the mystical body of thy Son, which is the blessed company of all faithful people; and are also heirs through hope of thy everlasting kingdom, by the merits of the most precious death and passion of thy dear Son. And we most humbly beseech thee, O heavenly Father, so to assist us with thy grace, that we may continue in that holy fellowship, and do all such good works as thou hast prepared for us to walk in; through Jesus Christ our Lord, to whom, with thee and the Holy Ghost, be all honour and glory, world without end. **AMEN**

We say together a hymn of praise, which has been used by Christians all over the world for hundreds of years; or we may stand and sing it.

Glory be to God on high, and in earth peace, goodwill towards men. We praise thee, we bless thee, we worship thee, we glorify thee, we give thanks to thee for thy great glory, O Lord God, heavenly King, God the Father Almighty.

O Lord, the only-begotten Son Jesu Christ; O Lord God, Lamb of God, Son of the Father, that takest away the sins of the world, have mercy upon us. Thou that takest away the sins of the world, have mercy upon us. Thou that takest away the sins of the world, receive our prayer. Thou that sittest at the right hand of God the Father, have mercy upon us.

For thou only art holy; thou only art the Lord; thou only, O Christ, with the Holy Ghost, art most high in the glory of God the Father. AMEN

The Priest ends the service with a blessing:
The peace of God, which passeth all understanding, keep your hearts and minds in the knowledge and love of God, and of his Son Jesus Christ our Lord: and the blessing of God Almighty, the Father, the Son, and the Holy Ghost, be amongst you and remain with you always. **AMEN**

We stand while the Priest and his assistants go out, and if the service is sung there will probably be a closing hymn.

Kneel again for a moment to thank God once more for allowing you to be there, and promise to show more of your love for Him in your daily life.

The Priest's Blessing.

Glossary

Words which refer to things used in the service, or which have changed their meaning since the Book of Common Prayer was written.

alb: long white garment worn by the celebrant and assistant clergy at Holy Communion, and often by lay assistants

brake: broke (the old past form of *break*)

bounden: obligatory

burse: square case which holds the corporal, covered in cloth of the colour of the season or festival

cassock: long garment, usually black, worn by clergy and lay assistants under the alb or surplice

celebrant: priest who conducts all or most of the Holy Communion and says the Prayer of Consecration

chalice: cup which holds the communion wine

chasuble: vestment worn by the celebrant over the alb, in the colour of the season or festival; it is like a sleeveless cloak passed over the head and hanging down in front and behind

ciborium: cup-shaped holder, usually with a lid, for the consecrated wafers

collect: short prayer said by the celebrant; there are set collects in the service, and a variable one for the season or festival

comfortable: strengthening and encouraging

corporal: square of linen placed on the altar under the chalice and paten at the offertory

council: once the close advisers of the Sovereign; now regarded as the Government and Members of Parliament

curate: parish priest; today generally refers to a junior priest in the parish, who should properly be called an 'assistant curate'

dalmatic: garment worn by a priest or deacon assisting at certain special services; it is a long tunic with short sleeves, in the same colour as the chasuble

frontal: cloth of the colour of the season or festival which hangs along the front of the altar

indifferently: impartially, without bias

lively: living and vital

magnify: praise

militant: the Church Militant is the Church of all living Christians, working for God in the world

oblation: offering; used both of the sacrifice of Christ on the Cross, and the offering of bread and wine in the service

offertory: the point in the service when the bread and wine are placed on the altar and the money gifts of the people are collected

pall: stiff piece of card covered with linen, placed on the chalice between the offertory and the consecration

paten: plate on which the bread is placed at the offertory and from which communion is given, unless a ciborium is used

property: nature, characteristic quality

quick: alive

stole: long piece of cloth passed behind the neck and hanging down on each side in front; worn under the chasuble and dalmatic, and over the surplice; a deacon wears the stole across the left shoulder; it is the same colour as the chasuble

substance: essential quality; used in the Creed to declare that Jesus Christ is truly God

surplice: white garment with sleeves, not as long as the alb, worn over the cassock

trespasses: sins

Testament: covenant; the New Testament in the Bible tells the story of God's promises to His faithful people

travail: hard and wearying work

tunicle: garment of the same shape as the dalmatic but worn without a stole

veil: square cloth, of the colour of the season or feast, placed over the chalice until the offertory